I0006324

PREFACE

Generative AI is not just another technological breakthrough—it's a force reshaping entire industries at an unprecedented pace. From revolutionizing patient care in healthcare to optimizing supply chains in manufacturing, from hyper-personalizing customer experiences in retail to reimagining financial services, this technology is driving a seismic shift in the way businesses operate. Yet, despite the hype, many organizations struggle to unlock its full potential.

"Transforming Industries with Generative AI" takes you on an insightful journey into the heart of this revolution, cutting through the noise to reveal what truly matters: how Generative AI is transforming businesses today, where the roadblocks lie, and what it takes to succeed in an AI-powered future.

Inside this book, you'll discover:

The Foundations of Generative AI: Unravel how this technology goes beyond automation, creating entirely new possibilities—whether it's AI-generated medical reports that reduce diagnostic errors or virtual fashion designers crafting personalized apparel.

Challenges and Untapped Potential: Why has Generative AI not yet fulfilled its promise? We'll explore real-world obstacles—like data biases, regulatory hurdles, and adoption hesitancy—and how businesses are overcoming them.

Industry Disruptions in Action: Learn from compelling case studies, such as how AI-driven drug discovery is slashing development timelines in pharmaceuticals or how major retailers like Amazon and Walmart are using AI to revolutionize inventory management and demand forecasting.

The Future of Work & Ethical Considerations: AI is changing the workforce—how can organizations reskill employees to work alongside AI? And how do we ensure AI-driven decisions remain ethical and unbiased?

This is not just a book about technology—it's a playbook for leaders, entrepreneurs, and professionals who want to stay ahead of the curve. Whether you're an executive trying to future-proof your business, a startup founder looking for a competitive edge, or an AI enthusiast eager to explore its real-world impact, this book will equip you with the insights and strategies to harness the full potential of Generative AI.

The AI revolution is here. Are you ready to lead it?

ABOUT THE AUTHOR

Nischal Kapoor is a seasoned technology executive and thought leader with over two decades of experience in driving innovation and digital transformation across various industries. As the author of "GenAI Made Easy: Harnessing Generative AI for Business Innovation," Nischal is dedicated to making complex AI concepts accessible to professionals and organizations seeking to leverage technology for growth.

With a background in IT strategy and implementation, Nischal has played a pivotal role in shaping the future of AI in business, helping organizations navigate the challenges and opportunities presented by emerging technologies.

In "Transforming Industries with Generative AI," Nischal shares his insights and expertise to guide readers through the transformative power of AI, inspiring them to embrace innovation and drive meaningful change within their organizations.

INTRODUCTION

Change is no longer an occasional disruption in business—it is the rhythm of the modern world. Entire industries are being reshaped overnight, and the companies that once led the market are now scrambling to keep up. Innovation is no longer a luxury; it is a necessity.

At the heart of this relentless transformation lies Artificial Intelligence (AI). For years, AI has promised to revolutionize industries, and in many ways, it already has. Automated customer service, predictive analytics, and data-driven decision-making have become essential tools for businesses worldwide. Yet, for all its progress, AI has mostly been about analysis—detecting patterns, optimizing operations, and improving efficiency.

But now, a new breed of AI has arrived—one that doesn't just analyze but creates.

The Rise of Generative AI

Generative AI marks a shift from prediction to invention. Unlike traditional AI, which processes existing data to identify trends, Generative AI produces entirely new content, ideas, and solutions. It can write articles, generate images, compose music, design products, and even develop new medical treatments. What was once the exclusive domain of human creativity is now being augmented—and in some cases, challenged—by AI.

In healthcare, Generative AI is designing molecules for life-saving drugs faster than any human researcher ever could. Companies like Insilico Medicine and DeepMind's AlphaFold have already shortened drug discovery timelines from years to months.

In retail, AI is creating hyper-personalized shopping experiences. Fashion brands like Nike and luxury retailers such as Gucci are using AI-generated designs to predict trends before they even emerge.

In manufacturing, companies like Boeing and Tesla are employing AI to generate optimized materials and streamline production, leading to lighter, stronger, and more efficient products.

In finance, AI is not just analyzing investments but generating risk models, personalized wealth strategies, and fraud-detection algorithms that evolve in real time.

In hospitality, AI is crafting unique, data-driven guest experiences, predicting customer preferences with uncanny accuracy, and even designing entire hotel interiors based on sentiment analysis.

These are not hypothetical scenarios. This is happening now.

From Hype to Reality

Yet, for all its promise, Generative AI has not yet fulfilled its potential.

Many businesses remain uncertain—intimidated by the complexity of AI, concerned about ethical risks, or unsure how to implement it in ways that actually drive value. The gap between AI's capabilities and its real-world application remains wide.

That's where this book comes in.

"Transforming Industries with Generative AI" is not a technical manual or a collection of abstract theories. It is a practical guide to understanding and leveraging Generative AI in the real world.

Through this book, you will:

1. Demystify Generative AI—breaking down how it works and why it matters in simple, clear language.
2. Explore real-world applications—with case studies and examples of how businesses across industries are using AI to transform operations and drive innovation.
3. Uncover the challenges and opportunities—examining why AI adoption is still slow in some industries and what companies can do to overcome barriers.
4. Gain strategic insights—providing business leaders, entrepreneurs, and professionals with the tools to implement Generative AI effectively and stay ahead of the competition.

The Future Belongs to Those Who Lead the AI Revolution

This isn't just a passing trend. AI is already shaping the businesses of the future. The question is no longer whether AI will disrupt industries—it's who will use it to lead that disruption.

Some will hesitate, waiting for clearer regulations, easier integrations, or a "perfect moment" that may never come. Others will seize the opportunity, leveraging Generative AI to create, innovate, and redefine what's possible.

The AI revolution is here. The only question left is: Will you be a part of it?

Turn the page, and let's begin.

GENERATIVE AI: THE PROMISE, THE REALITY, AND THE PATH FORWARD

The Anticipated Revolution

For years, Generative AI has been heralded as a game-changer—one that would redefine industries, drive innovation, and unlock unprecedented efficiencies. The emergence of powerful models like OpenAI's GPT series, Google's Gemini, and Anthropic's Claude fueled expectations of an AI-driven future where automation and creativity seamlessly blend to transform businesses.

The vision was grand: AI-powered systems generating marketing campaigns, automating customer interactions, designing products, and even revolutionizing fields like drug discovery and financial forecasting. Executives imagined a world where AI-driven insights would enhance decision-making, streamline operations, and elevate customer experiences.

Yet, as businesses have raced to adopt Generative AI, a stark reality has emerged—the technology has yet to fully deliver on its immense promise.

Why Generative AI Has Yet to Fulfill Its Potential

Despite its remarkable capabilities, Generative AI still faces significant hurdles. Businesses that rushed to integrate AI into their workflows have encountered unexpected challenges, revealing gaps between expectations and real-world outcomes.

1.Variability in Output Quality

While Generative AI can produce human-like text, code, and creative assets, its outputs often require extensive human oversight to ensure accuracy, context relevance, and brand alignment.

A 2023 Gartner report highlighted this challenge:
"While generative models show promise, their outputs often require significant refinement to meet business needs, reducing the efficiency gains they initially promised."

For organizations seeking AI-driven automation, the need for constant verification adds friction rather than reducing it.

AI-generated reports may lack industry-specific nuance, and marketing copy may require extensive revisions—diminishing the efficiency gains businesses expect.

2. Data Limitations and Model Bias

Generative AI is only as effective as the data it has been trained on. Poor-quality, outdated, or biased data can lead to misleading insights, unreliable outputs, and, in some cases, legal and reputational risks.

A Forrester Research study found that:
"Many organizations underestimate the role of high-quality data.

Without a robust data foundation, even the most advanced AI models will struggle to deliver real business value."

Companies relying on AI for decision-making must invest in data governance, quality control, and bias mitigation—or risk AI amplifying misinformation instead of improving insights.

3. Integration and Adoption Challenges

While AI promises to streamline operations, integrating it into existing business workflows remains a significant challenge. Outdated IT infrastructure, employee resistance, and lack of AI expertise can all hinder successful adoption.

A McKinsey report found that:
"Cultural resistance remains one of the top barriers to AI adoption, with 70% of organizations facing pushback from employees concerned about job displacement or overwhelmed by new technology."

True AI transformation requires more than just implementing new tools—it demands organizational alignment, upskilling employees, and rethinking workflows to maximize AI's value.

4. Ethical Concerns and Regulatory Uncertainty

The rise of Generative AI has raised pressing ethical questions, including bias in AI outputs, copyright disputes, and deepfake misinformation risks. Businesses adopting AI must navigate a complex landscape of evolving regulations, ethical considerations, and brand reputation concerns.

The World Economic Forum warns that:
"Organizations must proactively address AI ethics and governance to avoid regulatory scrutiny and reputational damage."

As regulations around AI-generated content, intellectual

property, and data privacy evolve, businesses must develop AI policies that prioritize transparency, fairness, and compliance to mitigate risk.

The Business Case for Generative AI Adoption

Despite these challenges, Generative AI remains one of the most transformative technologies of our time. Organizations that address its limitations strategically can unlock immense competitive advantages.

1. Unprecedented Efficiency and Productivity

Generative AI can automate repetitive tasks, freeing human talent for higher-value work. From AI-powered content creation to automated report generation, companies that embrace AI-driven efficiencies see measurable productivity gains.

A study by Accenture found that:
"Companies leveraging AI technologies experience a productivity boost of up to 40%. In customer support, AI automation has reduced response times by 25%, leading to higher customer satisfaction scores."

2. Enhanced Decision-Making with AI-Driven Insights

By analyzing vast amounts of structured and unstructured data, Generative AI can help leaders make smarter, faster decisions. AI-driven analytics provide deep insights into market trends, operational inefficiencies, and customer behavior.

According to a Harvard Business Review report:
"Organizations that effectively integrate AI-driven insights are 2.5

times more likely to make data-driven decisions that result in better business outcomes."

From finance to supply chain management, AI is becoming an indispensable tool for informed decision-making.

3. Personalization at Scale

Generative AI allows businesses to deliver hyper-personalized experiences—from tailored product recommendations to customized marketing campaigns.

A Deloitte study found that:
"Companies leveraging AI for personalized marketing strategies saw a 20% increase in customer retention and engagement."

In an era where consumers expect personalized experiences, AI enables brands to scale personalization without compromising efficiency.

4. Driving Innovation and Competitive Advantage

Generative AI doesn't just improve existing processes—it enables entirely new ways of doing business. AI-powered design, automated R&D, and real-time content generation are opening new revenue streams and market opportunities.

According to PwC's Global AI Study:
"65% of executives believe that AI will provide their companies with a significant competitive advantage within the next five years."

From AI-generated fashion designs to autonomous legal document drafting, early adopters of Generative AI are redefining their industries.

The Generative AI revolution is not inevitable—it is a choice.

While challenges remain, the businesses that proactively address AI's limitations and strategically integrate it into their operations will emerge as leaders in the new digital economy.

As AI analyst Chris Meserole aptly states:
"Generative AI is not just a passing trend—it's a pivotal technology reshaping industries. Organizations that invest in understanding and harnessing its potential today will define the future of business tomorrow."

The time to act is now. Will you embrace Generative AI as a transformative force, or risk being left behind?

THE EVOLUTION OF ARTIFICIAL INTELLIGENCE: FROM ANALYSIS TO CREATIVITY

The story of artificial intelligence is one of relentless evolution. Initially, AI was perceived as a powerful tool for data analysis —a system designed to identify patterns, predict outcomes, and automate routine tasks.

Businesses harnessed AI to extract valuable insights, reduce costs, and enhance efficiency. However, as the technology matured, AI's potential expanded beyond analytics, unlocking new realms of creativity and innovation. What was once the exclusive domain of human ingenuity has now become a collaborative effort between humans and machines.

At the heart of this transformation lies Generative AI. By shifting from analyzing data to creating entirely new content, AI has redefined the landscape of business innovation. Whether it's designing breakthrough products, generating compelling marketing content, or assisting in scientific discovery, Generative

AI is ushering in an era where artificial intelligence doesn't just predict the future—it helps shape it.

The Early Days: AI as a Data-Driven Tool

The origins of AI were deeply rooted in statistical analysis and automation. Businesses employed AI to process vast datasets and make informed predictions.

In industries like finance, retail, and healthcare, AI optimized workflows, managed inventories, and detected fraud. Machine learning, a subset of AI, enabled systems to learn from data over time, improving their ability to recognize images, interpret text, and provide accurate predictions.

However, these early AI models had inherent limitations. They excelled at structured data—numbers, records, and databases— but struggled with unstructured content such as images, videos, and text. AI's primary function was to analyze and predict, not to create. It could identify trends and forecast market movements, but it couldn't generate original ideas or devise entirely new strategies.

The real breakthrough arrived with the advent of deep learning, inspired by the neural architecture of the human brain. Deep learning algorithms, particularly neural networks, enabled AI to process unstructured data and recognize intricate patterns. This advancement paved the way for applications like facial recognition, real-time language translation, and self-driving technology. Yet, despite these innovations, AI remained predominantly analytical—until the emergence of Generative AI.

The Shift to Generative AI: Machines as Creators

Generative AI represents a fundamental shift in the role of

artificial intelligence. Instead of merely analyzing existing data, Generative AI models can create entirely new data that never existed before. This transformative ability sets Generative AI apart from its predecessors.

By learning patterns from vast datasets, Generative AI generates images, writes text, composes music, and even designs products, mimicking the creative process that was once thought to be uniquely human. Two key breakthroughs accelerated this evolution:

1. **Generative Adversarial Networks (GANs):** These AI models consist of two neural networks—a generator and a discriminator—that engage in a continuous feedback loop. The generator produces new data, while the discriminator evaluates its authenticity. Over time, the generator improves its outputs, ultimately creating highly realistic images, music, and other content.

2. **Transformer Models:** These advanced neural networks excel at processing and generating human-like text. Models such as OpenAI's GPT (Generative Pre-trained Transformer) and Google's BERT (Bidirectional Encoder Representations from Transformers) revolutionized AI-generated content, enabling more natural conversations, sophisticated content creation, and even code generation.

With these advancements, AI is no longer confined to interpretation and prediction—it actively contributes to creative processes, driving innovation across multiple industries.

Generative AI's Role in Business Innovation

The ability of AI to create is revolutionizing industries worldwide.

Instead of relying solely on human creativity, businesses now use AI as a collaborative partner, enhancing efficiency and accelerating innovation. Some of the most transformative applications include:

1. Product Design and Development

Generative AI is revolutionizing product design, allowing companies to create innovative solutions more efficiently.

- In automotive and aerospace industries, AI generates optimized designs for components, making them lighter, stronger, and more energy-efficient.
- In fashion and consumer goods, AI analyzes market trends and customer preferences to generate new clothing lines and accessories, reducing time-to-market and improving customer engagement.

2. Marketing and Content Creation

AI-driven content generation is changing the marketing landscape.

- Brands use AI to create personalized marketing campaigns, social media content, and product descriptions at scale.
- AI-powered chatbots enhance customer engagement by generating human-like responses, providing seamless support and personalized interactions.

3. Scientific Discovery and Innovation

Generative AI is accelerating advancements in pharmaceuticals and biotechnology.

- AI models analyze vast biological datasets to generate hypotheses, simulate experiments, and propose new drug compounds.
- AI-driven molecular design is expediting drug discovery,

significantly reducing research and development costs while improving treatment efficacy.

The Human-AI Collaboration

Despite its remarkable capabilities, Generative AI is not a replacement for human creativity—it is an enhancement. AI-generated content and designs still require human oversight, refinement, and strategic direction.

- In design and engineering, AI proposes multiple iterations, but human designers refine and validate the final versions.
- In marketing, AI produces drafts, but human professionals ensure the content aligns with brand identity and emotional resonance.

By working together, humans and AI can achieve groundbreaking innovations, blending computational efficiency with human ingenuity.

The Road Ahead for Generative AI

The transition from data-driven analysis to creative collaboration is only the beginning. As Generative AI continues to evolve, its applications will expand into new industries, from AI-generated art and music to AI-driven business strategies and personalized customer experiences.

In the following chapters, we will explore how specific industries are leveraging Generative AI to transform operations, enhance creativity, and redefine competitive advantages. From healthcare to manufacturing, Generative AI is not just shaping the future—it is creating it.

TRANSFORMING HEALTHCARE WITH GENAI

Healthcare is one of the industries where AI, particularly Generative AI, is poised to make the most profound and life-altering changes. While traditional AI applications have made strides in diagnostic imaging and predictive analytics, Generative AI takes innovation to another level by generating novel drugs, designing personalized treatment plans, and accelerating medical research and surgeries.

In this expanded chapter, we'll explore real-world applications of Generative AI in healthcare, supported by compelling data and case studies that highlight its transformative power.

AI's Role in Personalized Medicine

Generative AI is revolutionizing personalized medicine by enabling treatment plans tailored to individual patients' unique genetic, lifestyle, and environmental factors—moving away from the one-size-fits-all approach of traditional healthcare.

Tempus, a Chicago-based biotechnology firm, leverages AI and machine learning to build one of the world's largest libraries of clinical and molecular data.

The company utilizes this vast repository to generate personalized cancer treatment recommendations, factoring in genetic mutations, treatment history, and patient health records. In oncology—where highly customized therapies like chemotherapy and immunotherapy can make the difference between life and death—AI-driven insights are a game-changer.

Impact:
- A study on metastatic cancer patients found that those treated with AI-guided precision medicine strategies based on genetic mutations exhibited a **28% increase** in treatment response compared to standard treatment protocols.
- AI-driven pharmacogenomics, which analyzes genetic data to predict drug responses, has been shown to reduce adverse drug reactions and resistance by optimizing medication dosages based on a patient's liver enzyme profiles.
- A **2023 study in Nature Biotechnology** reported that AI-driven personalized medicine approaches led to a **35% reduction in hospital readmission rates** among oncology patients.
- Research by the **American Medical Association (AMA)** found that AI-generated personalized treatment plans improved outcomes for **60% of patients with rare genetic conditions**, surpassing conventional treatment methods.

AI-Driven Drug Discovery

Developing a new drug is traditionally a costly and time-consuming process, taking **10-15 years** and costing **$1-2 billion** per drug. With a clinical trial success rate of **less than 12%**, pharmaceutical companies face significant challenges. Generative AI is transforming this landscape by generating drug candidates and optimizing them for clinical trials, drastically reducing time and costs.

Insilico Medicine, a Hong Kong-based AI-driven biotechnology company, developed an AI model that successfully identified a novel drug candidate for **idiopathic pulmonary fibrosis (IPF)** in just **46 days**, a process that typically takes years.

The model generated new molecular structures and predicted their biological interactions, leading to a breakthrough in drug discovery.

- Insilico's AI reduced the preclinical drug discovery timeline by **74%**, cutting the process from **3-5 years** to less than a year.
- MIT researchers used a deep learning model to identify **Halicin**, a potent antibiotic effective against drug-resistant bacteria, discovering it from a pool of **100 million molecules** in just **days**.

Impact:

- The **Pharmaceutical Research and Manufacturers of America (PhRMA)** estimates that AI-driven drug discovery could save the industry up to **$70 billion annually** by reducing clinical trial failures and accelerating timelines.
- **McKinsey & Company** projects that AI-driven drug discovery could **reduce development costs by 20%** and **increase clinical trial success rates by 13%**.

Medical Imaging and Diagnostics

Radiology and pathology are undergoing a paradigm shift with AI-driven medical imaging. Traditional diagnostic methods are often time-consuming, subjective, and prone to human error.

Generative AI enhances imaging analysis, detects early disease markers, and simulates disease progressions, offering unparalleled diagnostic precision.

Zebra Medical Vision developed an AI system that analyzes X-rays, CT scans, and MRIs, flagging abnormalities like **lung nodules, fractures, and brain hemorrhages** with high accuracy.

- Zebra's AI detected lung nodules with a **92% accuracy rate**, surpassing the **85% accuracy of human radiologists**.
- The AI flagged potential findings **20% faster** than traditional analysis methods.

Google Health's deep learning model for **diabetic retinopathy** diagnoses retinal images with accuracy comparable to expert ophthalmologists.

- Google's AI achieved an **89% accuracy rate** in detecting diabetic retinopathy, outperforming local ophthalmologists in India by **26%**.

Impact:

- A **Frost & Sullivan report (2022)** projects that the global AI medical imaging market will grow from **$1.4 billion in 2022 to $4.7 billion by 2028**, reducing diagnostic errors by **up to 40%**.
- AI-assisted diagnostic imaging decreases radiologists' workload by **30%**, allowing them to focus on complex cases.

AI-Generated Treatment Plans

Generative AI is optimizing treatment planning in **oncology, cardiology, and neurology** by analyzing patient data and generating data-driven treatment strategies.

IBM Watson for Oncology

IBM Watson for Oncology analyzes medical literature and patient records to generate evidence-based treatment options for cancer patients.

- At **Manipal Hospitals in India,** Watson for Oncology's recommendations aligned with oncologists' decisions **96% of the time**.

PathAI for Pathology

PathAI developed an AI platform that analyzes digital pathology images, improving diagnostic accuracy and treatment planning for diseases like breast cancer.

- PathAI's AI algorithms improved diagnostic accuracy by **18%** and reduced false positives in breast cancer diagnoses by **24%**.

Impact:

- A **Journal of the American Medical Association (JAMA) study** found that AI-assisted treatment planning reduced hospital readmissions by **21%** and improved treatment adherence by **15%**.
- The **National Cancer Institute** reported that AI-driven precision medicine reduced **adverse treatment reactions by 32%**, leading to fewer hospitalizations.

AI-Enhanced Surgical Assistance

AI-powered robotic surgery systems are redefining precision, reducing complications, and accelerating patient recovery.

Intuitive Surgical's Da Vinci Robot

The **Da Vinci robotic system** enhances surgeons' precision in minimally invasive procedures, reducing incision size, recovery time, and complication rates.

- A **Lancet study** found that robotic-assisted surgeries using Da Vinci reduced complication rates by **27%** and shortened recovery times by **35%**.

Impact:

- The **global AI surgical robotics market** is projected to reach **$12.6 billion by 2026**.
- AI-assisted surgeries reduced **postoperative complication rates by 19%** and shortened hospital stays by **30%**, according to a **British Medical Journal study**.

Challenges and Ethical Considerations

Despite its promise, AI in healthcare presents challenges, including data privacy risks, algorithmic bias, and regulatory hurdles. AI models must be trained on diverse datasets to ensure equitable healthcare outcomes.

A **2021 Stanford University study** found that AI models used in dermatology were **40% less accurate** at detecting skin cancer in darker-skinned patients, highlighting the need for more inclusive training data.

Generative AI is redefining medicine, accelerating drug discovery, improving diagnostics, personalizing treatments, and enhancing surgical precision. However, ethical frameworks, regulatory oversight, and equitable AI adoption are crucial to ensuring that these innovations benefit all patients globally. As AI continues to evolve, its integration into healthcare promises to **save lives, reduce costs, and enhance patient care** on an unprecedented scale.

MANUFACTURING REVOLUTION WITH GENAI

Manufacturing has always been at the heart of economic growth and technological innovation, driving advances in efficiency, productivity, and product quality. Today, we stand at the threshold of another industrial revolution, one led by the power of Generative AI.

With this groundbreaking technology, manufacturing is shifting into the age of smarter factories, predictive maintenance, and fully automated supply chains. In this chapter, we'll explore how Generative AI is not just transforming production processes but also propelling the sector toward new frontiers in operational efficiency, innovation, and sustainability.

Generative Design: New Possibilities for Production

Generative design is one of the most impactful applications of Generative AI in manufacturing. By inputting design parameters —such as materials, performance requirements, and cost constraints—engineers can let AI generate a myriad of optimized design alternatives. This drastically reduces the time spent on design iterations, enables more innovative products, and results in lighter, stronger, and more efficient components.

General Motors (GM)

General Motors, in collaboration with Autodesk, used Generative AI to design car parts with groundbreaking results. When tasked with designing a new seatbelt bracket, the AI produced several alternative designs. The final product was 40% lighter and 20% stronger than the original. Moreover, the AI consolidated eight different components into one, simplifying assembly and cutting costs.

GM saw a 50% reduction in prototyping time for AI-generated components, which translated into faster vehicle production cycles and a reduction in material costs. The ability to accelerate design iteration and cut costs is a game changer in an industry that constantly faces competitive pressure.

Airbus

Airbus also leveraged Generative AI to redesign components for its A320 aircraft, with a focus on weight reduction and structural integrity. The AI generated cabin partition designs that were 45% lighter than traditional alternatives, a significant achievement considering the impact on fuel efficiency and operational costs.

Airbus estimated that these AI-generated designs saved 465,000 metric tons of CO_2 annually across its fleet by reducing fuel consumption. This not only lowered operational costs but also contributed to more sustainable manufacturing practices.

The Numbers Behind the Shift

- **Deloitte** reports that companies using AI-powered generative design have reduced time-to-market for new products by 30%.
- **PwC** found that manufacturers can achieve material cost

savings of up to 25% by using AI for optimized designs.

Predictive Maintenance: Reducing Downtime and Extending Machinery Lifespan

Generative AI is a key enabler of predictive maintenance—an area that can dramatically reduce unplanned downtimes, extend machinery life, and lower maintenance costs. Instead of relying on scheduled maintenance or reacting to failures after they occur, AI systems analyze real-time data to predict when a machine is likely to fail, allowing for preventative action.

Siemens

Siemens applied Generative AI in its gas turbine division to predict maintenance needs in real time. By analyzing sensor data from turbines, the AI could predict failures and alert the team to perform maintenance during non-peak hours. This approach minimized costly downtime and enhanced operational efficiency.

Siemens reported a 20% reduction in unplanned downtime and a 15% increase in overall equipment efficiency (OEE) as a result of AI-powered predictive maintenance.

Caterpillar

Caterpillar is another leader in predictive maintenance. Its AI models analyze real-time sensor data from machinery like excavators and bulldozers, predicting equipment failures before they happen. This allows customers to perform maintenance when it's most convenient, avoiding costly field breakdowns.

Caterpillar reduced machine downtime by 35%, resulting in a

22% improvement in fleet utilization and millions of dollars in savings for customers.

Insights

- **McKinsey** estimates that AI-driven predictive maintenance can reduce maintenance costs by 10% and cut downtime by up to 40%.
- **Accenture** found that manufacturers using AI for predictive maintenance reduced machinery failures by 70%, resulting in a 25% increase in operational efficiency.

AI-Driven Supply Chain Optimization: Creating Smarter, More Resilient Networks

Traditional supply chains are linear, with significant manual intervention needed to respond to demand fluctuations or disruptions. Generative AI is revolutionizing supply chain management by generating real-time insights and suggesting optimized strategies, making the entire system more dynamic and responsive.

Unilever

Unilever applied Generative AI to optimize its supply chain operations. The AI analyzed vast amounts of data—weather patterns, shipping costs, and consumer demand—allowing Unilever to adjust inventory and logistics strategies in real time. This dynamic approach helped prevent stockouts and ensured goods arrived on time.

Unilever's AI-powered system reduced inventory holding costs by 15%, improved on-time delivery by 20%, and boosted revenue by 5%.

Amazon

Amazon is a pioneer in using AI to optimize its supply chain. From predicting demand to generating optimal warehouse storage strategies and delivery routes, Amazon's AI-enabled logistics network ensures fast and efficient product delivery—even during peak times.

Amazon reduced shipping costs by 10% and sped up deliveries by 15%. AI also helped the company avoid stockouts, ensuring product availability during high-demand periods like Black Friday.

Benefits

- **BCG** reports that AI-driven supply chain optimizations have reduced costs by 12% and improved forecasting accuracy by 35%.
- **IDC** predicts that AI-enhanced supply chains will increase order fulfillment rates by up to 15%, reducing the risk of stockouts and overstocking.

Smart Factories: The Rise of Autonomous Production Systems

Generative AI is at the heart of the rise of smart factories. These factories are equipped with AI-powered systems that continuously monitor and optimize production, adjusting in real time to ensure maximum efficiency. These systems are capable of self-adjusting, minimizing waste, and enabling entirely automated production lines.

BMW

BMW's "Factory of the Future" integrates Generative AI into its production lines to streamline processes like assembly, welding, and painting. AI generates dynamic production schedules based on real-time resource availability, ensuring optimal production flow and reduced human error.

BMW reported a 20% improvement in production efficiency and

a 17% reduction in operational costs after implementing AI-powered automation, with a 15% reduction in material waste.

Foxconn

Foxconn, a global leader in electronics manufacturing, uses Generative AI to automate its smartphone assembly process. By continuously adjusting production parameters, the AI ensures smooth operations and minimizes errors on the factory floor.

Foxconn reduced production errors by 30%, increased worker productivity by 25%, and cut operational costs by 12% due to AI automation.

Key Statistics

- **Capgemini** found that AI-powered smart factories increase production output by 25% while reducing defect rates by up to 50%.
- **Gartner** forecasts that by 2027, 50% of large manufacturing companies will operate fully autonomous smart factories, cutting labor costs by 30% and scaling production.

AI-Enhanced Quality Control: Ensuring Precision and Consistency

Quality control remains a cornerstone of manufacturing success, but AI is taking this essential function to new heights. Generative AI helps predict defects and generate corrective actions in real time, ensuring that products meet the highest standards before they leave the factory.

Bosch

Bosch uses Generative AI to enhance quality control in automotive parts manufacturing. The AI system analyzes data from sensors and cameras to detect defects during production. If an issue is identified, the system generates immediate recommendations for corrective action.

Bosch achieved a 50% reduction in defective parts and a 25% improvement in the overall quality of automotive components with AI-powered quality control.

Nissan

Nissan implemented AI in its car manufacturing plants to improve quality control. The AI system monitors the production line for issues such as paint quality and component alignment, flagging potential problems before vehicles leave the assembly line.

Nissan saw a 22% reduction in defects and a 15% increase in overall vehicle quality ratings.

Impact in Numbers
- **Manufacturing.net** found that AI-driven quality control reduces production defects by 35%, cutting costs related to rework and warranty claims.
- **Deloitte** reports that AI in quality control improves customer satisfaction by 20% and boosts brand reputation with fewer defects and recalls.

Sustainability: AI's Role in Building a Greener Manufacturing Future

Generative AI is not only improving efficiency but also driving sustainability within manufacturing. By optimizing energy consumption, reducing waste, and improving resource management, AI is helping companies meet their sustainability goals without sacrificing productivity.

Schneider Electric

Schneider Electric used Generative AI to optimize energy consumption across its manufacturing plants. By generating real-time adjustments to production schedules and environmental systems, the company reduced energy consumption and carbon emissions.

Schneider Electric achieved a 25% reduction in energy consumption, saving $12 million annually while cutting CO_2 emissions by 42,000 metric tons.

Tesla

Tesla's Gigafactory utilizes AI to optimize both energy efficiency and material usage. By analyzing production processes, the AI ensures that energy use is minimized while maximizing material recycling rates.

Tesla's AI system cut energy usage by 15% and boosted material recycling by 18%.

Environmental Impact

- **World Economic Forum** reports that AI-driven sustainability measures can cut energy consumption by 20% and reduce waste by 30%.
- **IBM** shows that AI in resource management helps manufacturers reduce carbon emissions by up to 25%, making a significant contribution to global sustainability goals.

The Smart Manufacturing Revolution

Generative AI is not just transforming manufacturing—it is revolutionizing it. From generative design and predictive maintenance to AI-enhanced supply chains and smart factories, the possibilities for AI-driven innovation are vast.

Companies that embrace these technologies are seeing significant improvements in efficiency, cost reduction, and sustainability. The real-world examples and data in this chapter showcase how AI is not just a tool for operational excellence but a key driver of industry-wide transformation.

As we look to the future, it's clear that Generative AI will continue to play a central role in shaping manufacturing's evolution. This technology will enable companies to stay competitive, adapt to market demands, and build a more sustainable, efficient future

RETAIL REINVENTED WITH GENERATIVE AI

The retail industry is undergoing a profound transformation powered by Generative AI. From revolutionizing customer experiences to streamlining operational processes, AI is enabling retailers to improve efficiency, reduce costs, and engage customers in meaningful ways.

This chapter explores the ways Generative AI is reshaping the retail space, enhancing personalization, optimizing inventory management, and driving operational innovations.

Personalized Shopping Experiences

Generative AI is a game-changer in creating personalized shopping experiences for consumers. By analyzing vast amounts of customer data—including browsing behavior, purchase history, and preferences—AI can generate tailored product recommendations and marketing strategies that resonate on an individual level.

Amazon

Amazon employs sophisticated AI algorithms to track and analyze customer behavior, using that data to generate personalized product recommendations.

These suggestions are based on past purchases, items in the shopping cart, and even patterns observed in similar customers.

About 35% of Amazon's total revenue is attributed to its recommendation engine, underscoring the profound impact personalized marketing has on its business.

Stitch Fix

Stitch Fix, a subscription-based personal styling service, uses Generative AI to curate individualized clothing selections for customers.

By analyzing user preferences, style feedback, and fashion trends, the AI generates personalized clothing recommendations.

Stitch Fix boasts a customer retention rate exceeding 70%, a testament to the success of its AI-driven styling algorithms.

Impact

- McKinsey's research shows personalized marketing strategies can increase conversion rates by 10-30%.
- According to Segment, 71% of consumers feel frustrated when their shopping experience lacks personalization, further highlighting the importance of tailored approaches.

Optimizing Inventory Management

Inventory management remains a critical challenge for retailers, with the need to balance demand and supply while minimizing overstock and understock situations. Generative AI addresses these challenges by forecasting demand, optimizing stock levels, and automating replenishment processes.

Walmart

Walmart uses AI to analyze massive data sets, including sales trends, local weather, and even local events, to predict product demand. These insights help managers adjust inventory levels for each store, reducing shortages and overstock situations.

AI implementation at Walmart has led to a 15% reduction in out-of-stock instances and a 25% decrease in excess inventory.

Zara

Zara, a fast-fashion retailer, employs AI to optimize inventory management by analyzing purchase data and customer trends. This allows Zara to more accurately forecast which products should be produced and stocked at specific locations.

Zara saw a 20% reduction in stock turnover and a 30% boost in sales through more efficient inventory management.

Impact

- Deloitte's findings show that AI-driven inventory optimization can reduce stock-outs by 40% and decrease excess inventory by 30%.
- Gartner estimates that AI-enhanced inventory management can lead to a 20-25% improvement in sales forecasting accuracy.

AI-Driven Supply Chain Optimization

Generative AI's ability to analyze data across an entire supply chain—from suppliers to distribution centers to retail outlets —helps businesses improve logistics, reduce lead times, and enhance overall supply chain performance.

Target

Target uses AI to optimize its supply chain logistics by analyzing traffic patterns, delivery schedules, and inventory needs to identify the most efficient routes for product delivery.

Target has reduced logistics costs by 15% and improved delivery speed by 20% through AI-driven supply chain optimizations.

The Home Depot

The Home Depot applies AI to streamline its supply chain, analyzing customer demand, inventory levels, and product sourcing. This leads to enhanced product distribution and order fulfillment.

The Home Depot achieved a 10% reduction in supply chain costs and a 25% improvement in order fulfillment rates.

Impact

- Capgemini's research shows that AI-powered supply chain optimization can improve order fulfillment rates by 15% and reduce logistics costs by 10-20%.
- McKinsey notes that retailers using AI in supply chain management have experienced up to a 30% reduction in lead times and a 15% improvement in inventory turnover.

Enhancing Customer Engagement with AI Chatbots

Generative AI-powered chatbots are revolutionizing customer engagement by providing instant, round-the-clock support, assisting with product recommendations, and answering customer inquiries. The more these bots interact with users, the more adept they become at responding to specific needs.

Sephora

Sephora leverages AI-driven chatbots on its website and mobile app to offer personalized beauty product recommendations and assist with queries related to skincare and cosmetics.

Sephora reported a 30% increase in customer engagement and a 20% boost in sales from its AI chatbot interactions.

H&M

H&M uses AI chatbots to improve customer service by providing real-time answers about product availability, store locations, and order statuses.

Since implementing AI chatbots, H&M has reduced customer service response times by 25% and improved customer satisfaction by 15%.

Impact

- IBM research suggests that businesses using AI chatbots can reduce customer service costs by 30%.
- Oracle reports that 80% of businesses plan to use AI chatbots by 2025, emphasizing the growing importance of AI in customer engagement.

Dynamic Pricing Strategies

Generative AI enables retailers to implement dynamic pricing by analyzing competitor pricing, demand fluctuations, and market conditions. AI can provide real-time pricing adjustments that optimize revenue without alienating customers.

Uber

Uber's AI system adjusts pricing dynamically based on real-time demand and supply, ensuring availability during peak times while maximizing revenue.

Uber reported a 20% revenue increase during peak times due to its AI-powered dynamic pricing model.

Ticketmaster

Ticketmaster uses Generative AI to adjust ticket prices based on demand for specific events. The AI analyzes historical sales data and current demand to optimize ticket pricing.

Ticketmaster saw a 15% increase in revenue for events using AI-based dynamic pricing compared to traditional pricing methods.

Impact

- McKinsey's study reveals that AI-driven dynamic pricing can result in a 5-10% revenue increase.
- Deloitte notes that businesses using AI for pricing strategies report a 15% improvement in profit margins.

Leveraging AI for In-Store Experiences

Generative AI is also transforming in-store experiences, helping retailers design spaces that attract customers and encourage purchases. By analyzing customer behavior, AI provides insights into store layout optimization and product placement.

Lowe's

Lowe's utilizes AI to analyze customer traffic patterns and preferences, adjusting store layouts and product placements to maximize visibility and sales.

Lowe's reported a 10% sales increase for products placed based on AI-derived insights.

Macy's

Macy's uses AI to enhance in-store experiences with personalized promotions and targeted marketing, offering customers tailored deals as they shop.

Macy's achieved a 15% increase in in-store sales by implementing AI-driven personalized marketing.

Impact

- Retail Dive reports that AI-driven in-store experiences can improve customer retention by 20%.
- Forrester's research shows that personalized in-store experiences can increase transaction values by 15%.

AI and Sustainability in Retail

As sustainability becomes a key priority for consumers, Generative AI is helping retailers reduce waste, optimize resource use, and improve sustainability efforts.

Unilever

Unilever employs AI to streamline its supply chain and reduce waste, resulting in better recycling and more sustainable packaging choices.

Unilever reduced its plastic usage by 25% across its product packaging through AI-driven sustainability strategies.

IKEA

IKEA uses AI to optimize material sourcing and product lifecycle analysis to create more sustainable products and reduce waste.

IKEA reduced supply chain waste by 20% through its AI-powered sustainability efforts.

Impact

- Accenture reports that AI-driven sustainability initiatives can reduce carbon emissions by 30%.
- The World Economic Forum indicates that AI-based sustainability strategies can increase consumer loyalty by 25%.

A New Era for Retail

Generative AI is rapidly reshaping the retail industry, enhancing customer engagement, optimizing operational processes, and driving sustainability.

The examples and data provided in this chapter highlight the transformative potential of AI, emphasizing its role in creating personalized, efficient, and sustainable retail experiences.

Retailers that adopt Generative AI will be well-positioned to thrive in a competitive and ever-evolving marketplace.

REINVENTING FINANCIAL SERVICES WITH GENERATIVE AI

In the ever-evolving financial services sector, **Generative AI** is making waves by not only **optimizing operations** but also enhancing **customer experiences** and improving **risk management**.

As we explore the future of banking, insurance, and investment services, AI is fostering innovation and creating **unprecedented efficiencies**.

AI-Enhanced Customer Service in Banking

Customer service remains a cornerstone of the banking industry, and Generative AI is paving the way for faster, more personalized interactions. From AI chatbots to virtual assistants, financial institutions are leveraging AI to streamline customer service, answering inquiries in real-time and even assisting with complex transactions.

Bank of America - Erica

Bank of America's AI-powered virtual assistant, **Erica**, is revolutionizing customer interactions. With over 15 million users, Erica provides tailored banking experiences, from answering customer queries to offering insightful financial advice based on behavior patterns.

With more than 140 million client requests handled, Erica has **boosted customer engagement** significantly.

Capital One - Eno

Capital One's **Eno** helps customers track their spending and manage transactions through AI-driven conversations, delivering personalized offers.

25% increase in customer satisfaction since Eno's introduction shows how AI-driven interactions elevate experience.

Insights:
- AI chatbots can save banks up to **$7.3 billion annually** by 2023 (Juniper Research).
- 63% of customers prefer interacting with **AI chatbots** for basic inquiries (PwC Survey).

Risk Management and Fraud Detection

AI is fundamentally changing how financial institutions detect and mitigate fraud and manage risk. By analyzing vast datasets and identifying patterns, Generative AI is enhancing security and response times.

JPMorgan Chase - Fraud Detection

JPMorgan Chase utilizes **AI algorithms** to monitor transactions in real time, promptly identifying suspicious activities and preventing fraud before it escalates.

AI-powered systems helped **reduce fraud losses by 25%**, showcasing the power of predictive analytics in fraud detection.

Mastercard - AI in Fraud Prevention

Mastercard's AI system analyzes transaction data and identifies fraudulent activity by spotting unusual spending patterns, often blocking suspicious transactions in real-time.

$7 billion in fraud attempts were **prevented** through their AI-driven fraud detection.

Insights:

- Organizations using AI for fraud detection can reduce detection time by up to **90%** (ACFE).
- AI-driven risk management can lower operational risks by **30%** (Capgemini).

Investment Management and Wealth Advisory

AI is reshaping investment management and wealth advisory, allowing clients to make more informed decisions. By analyzing market trends and portfolio performance, AI is driving personalized investment strategies.

BlackRock - AI for Investment Strategies

BlackRock uses AI to analyze vast amounts of market data and generate insights for investment strategies, ultimately enhancing decision-making for clients.

AI-driven insights contributed to a **15% increase** in investment performance.

Wealthfront - Automated Investment Management

Wealthfront leverages AI to automate investment services,

providing tailored portfolios based on clients' unique profiles and market conditions.

Wealthfront has experienced **30% growth** in assets under management.

Insights:

- Firms using AI in investment management achieve **10-20% higher portfolio returns** (Deloitte).
- AI wealth management services can reduce operational costs by up to **30%** (McKinsey).

Regulatory Compliance and Reporting

Navigating complex regulations is one of the toughest challenges in the financial services industry, but AI is stepping in to automate processes and ensure compliance. AI can analyze ever-changing regulations and generate real-time compliance reports.

HSBC - Streamlining Compliance

HSBC uses AI to streamline its compliance processes by analyzing transaction data and generating reports that meet regulatory standards.

HSBC reduced **compliance costs by 20%** with AI-powered compliance tools.

Deloitte - AI in Regulatory Reporting

Deloitte's AI system automates regulatory reporting, improving the accuracy of reports and reducing the burden of manual work.

- **Impact**: Deloitte saw a **30% increase** in efficiency in their regulatory reporting processes.

Insights:

- Financial institutions using AI for compliance can reduce compliance costs by up to **50%** (Accenture).
- AI-driven regulatory reporting can improve **accuracy by 40%**, minimizing risks (PwC).

The Future of Financial Services

Generative AI is not just transforming financial services; it is redefining them. By improving customer engagement, enhancing risk management, optimizing investment strategies, and streamlining compliance processes, AI is becoming an indispensable tool for innovation impact across various financial services, one thing is certain: the future of finance is powered by AI

REVOLUTIONIZING HOSPITALITY WITH GENERATIVE AI

The hospitality industry is undergoing a radical shift, with Generative AI at the forefront of innovation. From enhancing guest experiences to optimizing operations and driving marketing strategies, AI is reshaping the way hotels, restaurants, and other hospitality services operate. This chapter delves into how AI is driving efficiencies and elevating guest satisfaction across the sector.

Enhancing Guest Experiences

Generative AI is revolutionizing the guest experience by delivering personalized interactions and instant support. With the ability to analyze guest data, AI tailors services to individual preferences, ensuring high satisfaction and fostering loyalty.

Marriott International

Marriott integrates AI into its mobile app to enhance guest personalization. The AI analyzes previous stay data and guest preferences, offering tailored room features, amenities, and local experiences.

Marriott reported a 20% increase in guest satisfaction after introducing AI-driven personalization in their app.

Hilton

Hilton uses an AI-powered chatbot to offer instant customer service. Guests can interact with the chatbot for bookings, inquiries, and room service requests, reducing wait times.

Hilton's AI chatbot reduced response times by 60%, resulting in a 15% increase in overall guest satisfaction.

Impact:

- **30% Increase in Loyalty:** According to Deloitte, personalized guest experiences can boost customer loyalty by up to 30%.
- **80% Preference for Personalized Stays:** Oracle's report shows that 80% of guests are more likely to return to hotels offering personalized experiences.

Optimizing Operations and Efficiency

Generative AI is enhancing operational efficiency by optimizing staffing, managing resources, and streamlining booking processes. AI algorithms analyze data to predict trends and improve decision-making, ultimately boosting performance.

Accor Hotels

Accor uses AI to forecast booking trends and predict peak occupancy periods, helping to optimize staffing levels and reduce labor costs.

AI-driven staffing optimization led to a 25% reduction in labor costs at Accor.

Hyatt Hotels

Hyatt leverages AI to analyze guest behavior, enhancing its booking system and marketing strategies. This AI-driven solution provides insights that help increase conversion rates.

Hyatt saw a 20% rise in online bookings after implementing AI-powered website and booking system enhancements.

Impact:

- **15-25% Reduction in Costs:** McKinsey found that AI can help hotels cut operational costs by 15-25%.
- **30% Improvement in Efficiency:** A study by Cornell University shows that AI-driven resource management boosts operational efficiency by up to 30%.

Streamlining Marketing Strategies

Generative AI is transforming marketing in hospitality by delivering insights for targeted campaigns and personalized promotions. By analyzing customer data, AI tailors marketing efforts that resonate with potential guests, driving bookings and engagement.

Booking.com

Booking.com employs AI to analyze customer search patterns and preferences, enabling personalized marketing campaigns. The AI suggests tailored promotions and recommendations to enhance user engagement.

AI-powered marketing campaigns resulted in a 35% increase in conversion rates at Booking.com.

Expedia

Expedia uses AI to personalize travel recommendations, analyzing user behavior to optimize offers.

Expedia's AI-driven marketing increased customer engagement by 25%.

Impact:

- **10-20% Increase in Booking Rates:** Salesforce reports that personalized marketing increases booking rates for hospitality businesses by 10-20%.
- **70% Preference for Personalization:** Statista found that 70% of travelers prefer personalized offers from hotels and travel providers.

Driving Operational Analytics and Insights

Generative AI enables hotels to make data-driven decisions by analyzing vast amounts of operational data, providing valuable insights for strategic planning and improved performance.

InterContinental Hotels Group (IHG)

IHG uses AI for operational analytics, examining guest preferences and occupancy trends to optimize pricing and promotional strategies.

IHG reported a 20% increase in revenue per available room (RevPAR) after implementing AI-powered pricing optimization.

Wyndham Hotels

Wyndham uses AI to analyze guest feedback, identifying patterns that inform service quality improvements and staff training.

Wyndham's use of AI in service quality enhancements resulted in a 15% improvement in guest satisfaction ratings.

Impact:

- **25% Increase in Profitability:** Deloitte reports that data-driven decision-making boosts hospitality profitability by 25%.

- **Improved Service Offerings:** PwC's research highlights that AI-driven analytics enhance customer insights, leading to better service offerings.

The Future of Hospitality

Generative AI is revolutionizing the hospitality landscape by enhancing guest experiences, optimizing operations, and driving innovative marketing strategies. The case studies and data presented in this chapter illustrate how AI leads to increased revenue, reduced operational costs, and higher customer satisfaction.

As more hospitality businesses adopt AI technologies, they can expect to not only improve their bottom line but also foster customer loyalty through personalized services and innovative solutions. The future of hospitality lies in leveraging the power of AI to create unforgettable experiences, streamline operations, and drive continuous innovation in the sector.

OVERCOMING CHALLENGES IN AI IMPLEMENTATION

Addressing Data Privacy and Security Risks in AI Adoption

As AI technologies are increasingly integrated into organizational processes, the associated risks to data privacy and security grow significantly.

The collection and processing of sensitive personal data through AI systems raise concerns about data breaches, non-compliance with regulations like GDPR and HIPAA, and overall vulnerability to cyberattacks.

Example: Data Breach in Healthcare

In 2020, a major healthcare provider, Universal Health Services, experienced a significant data breach, exposing the personal information of over 3 million patients. The breach, caused by inadequate security protocols, resulted in severe reputation damage and a $2 million fine.

This highlights the critical importance of strong data security measures as organizations adopt AI technologies.

Key Security Measures for AI-Driven Solutions

To mitigate data privacy and security risks, organizations must implement robust data governance frameworks, with particular focus on the following strategies:

1. **Encryption:**
   Encrypting sensitive data both during transmission and when stored is essential for preventing unauthorized access. A 2023 study by Cybersecurity Ventures found that organizations using encryption saw a 50% reduction in successful data breaches, making it a key tool for AI adoption.

2. **Access Controls:**
   Implementing multi-factor authentication and access controls ensures that only authorized individuals can access sensitive data. According to Gartner, organizations with strong access control measures experienced a 70% reduction in internal data breaches, making it a critical aspect of AI security.

3. **Regular Audits:**
   Performing regular security audits is necessary for identifying and addressing potential vulnerabilities in data-handling processes. A PwC study revealed that 84% of organizations that conducted routine audits reported higher compliance with data protection regulations, leading to a more secure AI environment.

Overcoming Organizational Barriers to AI Adoption

Despite AI's transformative potential, many organizations face internal resistance to its adoption. Employees may fear job displacement, and outdated infrastructure can complicate the successful integration of AI technologies.

Survey Insights:

A McKinsey survey showed that 70% of organizations encounter cultural barriers when implementing AI, while 60% identify outdated IT infrastructure as a significant hurdle. These challenges often arise from a lack of understanding of AI's potential to enhance roles rather than replace them.

Strategies for Overcoming Resistance

Organizations can take several approaches to reduce resistance and foster a culture of innovation:

1. **Promote Transparency:**
   Clearly communicating the benefits of AI to employees and involving them in the process can help alleviate fears. Research from Deloitte shows that companies that actively involve employees in AI initiatives experience a 30% increase in buy-in, creating a smoother adoption process.
2. **Engage Leadership:**
   Securing support from leadership is crucial for AI adoption. A case study by IBM demonstrated that organizations with strong executive sponsorship for AI initiatives were 2.5 times more likely to succeed compared to those without such backing.
3. **Start with Pilot Programs:**
   Introducing AI through smaller pilot programs can allow employees to witness the benefits without overwhelming them with sweeping changes. For example, Coca-Cola's implementation of an AI-driven marketing tool as a pilot resulted in a 10% increase in campaign effectiveness, proving the value of starting small before scaling.

Mitigating Risks and Ensuring Smooth AI Integration

To address both data security concerns and organizational challenges, businesses need a clear framework for AI adoption that includes robust risk management and strategic planning.

1. **Comprehensive Risk Assessment:**
   Conducting detailed risk assessments helps organizations identify data privacy vulnerabilities before implementing AI. For example, a financial institution analyzed potential compliance risks before implementing an AI-driven fraud detection system, allowing them to address vulnerabilities proactively and avoid costly fines.

2. **Effective Change Management:**
   Successful AI adoption requires managing the cultural shifts that come with new technology. Retail companies, for instance, have seen smoother transitions when they implement structured change management strategies. One large retailer experienced a 40% reduction in employee turnover during AI implementation by supporting staff throughout the transition.

3. **Employee Training Programs:**
   Training employees to use AI tools effectively is crucial for maximizing their potential. For example, a manufacturing company that introduced AI-driven automation tools reported a 25% increase in productivity after providing employees with tailored AI training programs, highlighting the importance of developing internal capabilities for AI integration.

Case Study: Fraud Detection in Financial Services

A global financial institution implemented an AI-powered fraud detection system. By conducting comprehensive risk assessments and providing employee training, they were able to reduce fraudulent transactions by 40% within the first year, saving an estimated $1.5 million in fraud-related losses.

NAVIGATING THE FUTURE OF AI IN BUSINESS

AI adoption comes with significant security and cultural challenges, but organizations can successfully mitigate these risks by embracing encryption, access controls, regular audits, and a transparent approach to change management.

With the right strategies in place, businesses can unlock AI's transformative potential, improving both operational efficiency and customer satisfaction, while safeguarding sensitive data.

The future of AI integration hinges on overcoming these challenges, ensuring that businesses can fully capitalize on the opportunities AI presents without compromising security or employee buy-in

AI and the Workforce: Reskilling for the Future

The Evolving Roles of Employees in an AI-Driven World

The rapid advancement of artificial intelligence (AI) is transforming industries and reshaping job roles in ways that were once unimaginable.

As AI becomes increasingly integrated into everyday business operations, tasks that were once performed by humans—especially those that are routine and repetitive—are now being automated.

But AI's impact extends far beyond automation. It is fundamentally changing how work is conceptualized and carried out, placing a greater emphasis on creativity, strategy, and problem-solving.

AI is no longer just a tool that drives efficiency; it is an agent of transformation, redefining the roles of employees across industries.

No longer are workers solely expected to follow a set of

instructions or perform manual labor. Instead, employees must focus on tasks that require emotional intelligence, critical thinking, and complex decision-making—skills that are uniquely human.

According to a report by the World Economic Forum, 85 million jobs may be displaced due to the shift from human labor to machine-driven processes by 2025. However, this disruption comes with a silver lining. The same report projects that

97 million new roles will emerge, driven by the growing demand for AI, data analysis, machine learning expertise, and AI ethics. These new roles will not only replace the jobs lost but will also require entirely different skill sets, emphasizing the need for workers to be prepared for the future of work.

This shift represents a massive opportunity for organizations and workers alike, but it requires a concerted effort to bridge the skills gap and ensure that employees are equipped with the capabilities they need to thrive in the AI-driven landscape.

Strategies for Upskilling and Reskilling the Workforce

To fully harness the potential of AI and ensure that employees remain relevant in a rapidly changing job market, organizations must prioritize continuous learning and development.

This investment in upskilling and reskilling is not only crucial for maintaining competitiveness but also for fostering a workforce that is adaptable, resilient, and capable of navigating the AI revolution.

Key strategies for preparing the workforce for AI-driven change include:

1. **Skill Gap Analysis:**
   Conducting regular assessments to identify the skills employees currently possess and those required for the future is essential for effective training programs. Companies like Siemens have successfully leveraged skill gap analysis to tailor their training initiatives, resulting in a 20% increase in employee competency in emerging technologies such as AI and machine learning. Skill gap analysis allows organizations to ensure that their workforce is equipped to meet the demands of the future.

2. **Customized Training Programs:**
   A one-size-fits-all approach to training will not suffice in an era where industries and technologies are evolving at an unprecedented pace. Companies must offer tailored training programs that focus on the skills most relevant to the organization's specific AI initiatives. For example, a major tech company implemented a customized program that focused on AI ethics and compliance, reducing compliance-related incidents by 15%. These programs can help employees stay ahead of the curve by learning the exact skills required to thrive in their roles.

3. **Mentorship and Knowledge Sharing:**
   Establishing mentorship programs that pair experienced employees with those new to AI technologies is an effective way to foster a culture of knowledge sharing. AT&T launched such a mentorship initiative, resulting in a 30% increase in employee retention among those involved. Mentorship not only accelerates learning but also helps employees build a sense of community and shared

purpose, which can be particularly valuable in industries undergoing significant change.

4. **Continuous Feedback and Adaptation:**
AI tools evolve rapidly, and so must the employees using them. Organizations should create mechanisms for ongoing feedback to ensure that training programs remain relevant. A continuous feedback loop helps organizations adjust their approaches and adapt their training to meet evolving technological needs. For instance, tech companies are increasingly adopting agile learning environments where feedback from employees is integrated into training design, ensuring that employees stay ahead of the curve in mastering AI-related skills.

Case Study: Workforce Transformation in AI-Powered Industries

Consider the case of a large manufacturing company that launched a comprehensive reskilling initiative aimed at integrating AI technologies into its operations. The company provided employees with training in data analytics and AI-powered tools that would directly impact their work. The results were striking:

- **Increased Productivity:**
Employees who participated in the program saw a 20% increase in production efficiency. The reskilling initiative helped employees become more proficient with AI-assisted workflows, which reduced the time spent on manual tasks and improved the accuracy of their work. Productivity gains were particularly notable in areas such as supply chain optimization, where AI-powered algorithms were used to streamline processes.

- **Enhanced Confidence and Engagement:**
Of the employees who underwent the training, 75% reported feeling more confident in their ability to work

with AI tools, and this sense of competence translated into increased engagement. As workers became more adept at leveraging AI to enhance their workflows, they were more willing to take on complex challenges and contribute innovative ideas. This boost in confidence played a significant role in the company's ability to integrate AI without significant resistance.

- **Employee Retention and Satisfaction:**
A survey conducted post-training revealed a 40% improvement in employee satisfaction, particularly among those who participated in the upskilling program. Workers felt empowered by their newfound skills, leading to improved morale and a more collaborative work environment. When employees perceive that their employers are invested in their growth and development, they are more likely to remain with the organization, reducing turnover.

AI in the Healthcare Industry: A Look at Reskilling for AI Adoption

In the healthcare industry, the adoption of AI has been particularly transformative. AI-driven tools are helping doctors diagnose diseases with greater accuracy, and hospitals are using AI to streamline administrative tasks and improve patient care. However, for these innovations to be effective, healthcare professionals must receive the necessary training.

One notable example is the partnership between a major hospital network and a leading AI provider.

The network launched a specialized reskilling program to train its medical staff in using AI for diagnostics, patient management, and data analysis. Within six months, the hospital saw:

- **15% increase in diagnostic accuracy** using AI-powered tools, reducing misdiagnosis rates.
- **20% improvement in patient outcomes**, thanks to AI's ability to assist doctors in making faster and more accurate decisions.

These results underscore the value of investing in AI education and training for employees, particularly in sectors like healthcare, where lives are on the line.

The Road Ahead: A Future of AI-Enhanced Workforces

The shift towards an AI-powered world is inevitable, and as organizations navigate this transition, it's clear that reskilling and upskilling the workforce are not merely options—they are imperatives.

The rise of AI presents both challenges and opportunities. By investing in continuous learning, offering customized training, and fostering a culture of innovation, organizations can ensure that their workforce remains adaptable, skilled, and ready to take on the jobs of tomorrow.

As we move into a future where humans and machines work in tandem, employees will no longer be seen as simply workers but as creators, strategists, and problem-solvers—capable of leveraging AI to enhance human potential rather than replace it. In this new world of work, the key to success will lie in the ability of organizations to equip their people with the tools and knowledge they need to thrive in an AI-driven environment.

The Future of Generative AI in Business: Transforming Industries and Unlocking New Potential

Emerging Trends in AI Technology

As Generative AI continues to evolve, its profound impact on businesses across industries is becoming more evident. While the technology has already revolutionized various sectors, the coming years promise even greater advancements.

Here are the key trends that will shape the future of Generative AI in business:

1. **Increased Collaboration Between Humans and AI:**
   One of the most exciting shifts in AI's evolution is its transition from a tool to a collaborative partner. AI will not replace human creativity or decision-making but will instead enhance them. This collaboration between humans and AI will lead to breakthroughs in fields ranging from design and marketing to healthcare and finance. According to Accenture, companies that promote human-AI collaboration experience up to a 40% increase in productivity. By leveraging AI to handle routine tasks and process large volumes of data, employees will have more time to focus on high-level creativity, complex problem-solving, and strategic thinking.

2. **AI Ethics and Governance:**
   As AI becomes more integrated into business processes, ethical considerations are taking center stage. Organizations must ensure that AI systems operate fairly and without bias, and establish frameworks for governance that promote transparency and accountability. According to a Deloitte survey, 78% of executives recognize that ethical AI will be central to their AI strategies in the coming years. As AI's role in decision-making grows, businesses will need to adopt clear policies to

address issues related to data privacy, bias, fairness, and accountability. By doing so, they will not only reduce risks but also build trust with customers and stakeholders.

3. **Real-Time Decision Making:**
   The ability to make real-time decisions based on data is a critical advantage in today's fast-paced market. AI's ability to analyze vast amounts of data instantly and predict outcomes will revolutionize industries by improving responsiveness to market changes and customer needs. A logistics company that integrated AI-driven systems for route optimization saw a 15% reduction in delivery times, underscoring the power of AI to drive operational efficiency. In industries like finance, healthcare, and retail, real-time decision-making powered by AI will enable businesses to stay agile and competitive in an increasingly dynamic environment.

HOW BUSINESSES CAN STAY AHEAD IN THE AI RACE

To stay competitive in the rapidly evolving AI landscape, businesses must take proactive steps to integrate AI into their operations. Here are strategies that organizations can adopt to stay ahead of the curve:

1. **Invest in Research and Development:**
   AI is still in its early stages, and the potential for new applications is vast. To stay ahead, businesses must dedicate resources to research and development (R&D) to explore innovative AI solutions that can drive growth and efficiency. Amazon, for example, invests heavily in AI research, particularly in the areas of supply chain optimization and customer experience. This investment has led to transformative advancements, including AI-powered recommendation engines and highly efficient warehouse robots. By prioritizing R&D, businesses can uncover new ways to leverage AI to gain a competitive edge.

2. **Foster a Culture of Innovation:**
   The rapid pace of AI development means that companies must be agile and willing to experiment. Google's famous

"20% time" policy, which allows employees to spend a portion of their workweek on innovative projects, has led to the creation of groundbreaking products like Gmail and Google Maps. By encouraging experimentation and embracing a culture of risk-taking, companies can foster the kind of innovation that leads to AI-driven breakthroughs. Companies that empower employees to think creatively and take ownership of AI projects will be better positioned to adapt to new technological advancements.

3. **Collaborate with AI Technology Providers:**
Partnering with AI technology providers can accelerate the implementation of AI solutions by providing businesses with access to cutting-edge tools, expertise, and resources. For example, retailers who collaborate with AI firms to develop personalized customer experiences have seen significant improvements in engagement and sales. AI technology providers can also offer businesses valuable insights into best practices for AI adoption and help navigate challenges related to integration, training, and scaling. By working with external partners, businesses can tap into the full potential of AI and expedite their digital transformation.

THE ROLE OF INNOVATION ECOSYSTEMS

The future of AI in business will be shaped not just by individual companies but by collaborative ecosystems that foster innovation and knowledge-sharing.

These ecosystems bring together businesses, AI developers, researchers, and thought leaders to drive the next generation of AI technologies. By participating in innovation ecosystems, organizations can stay at the forefront of AI developments and benefit from the collective expertise of the community.

One example of an innovation ecosystem is the growing network of AI research labs, academic institutions, and private-sector companies working together to solve AI-related challenges.

In industries like healthcare, automotive, and manufacturing, companies that engage with these ecosystems have been able to implement AI solutions more effectively and develop new products and services that otherwise would not have been possible.

A retail company partnered with an AI technology provider

to develop a personalized shopping experience using machine learning algorithms. The initiative resulted in a 25% increase in customer engagement and a 15% boost in sales within six months. This success story underscores the tangible benefits of AI integration and highlights the importance of collaborating with AI technology providers to bring innovative solutions to market.

A CALL TO ACTION FOR INDUSTRY LEADERS

As the AI-driven future unfolds, industry leaders must act now to position their organizations for success. The integration of AI into business operations is no longer a distant goal—it's an urgent necessity. Organizations that fail to adopt AI will be left behind, while those that embrace the technology will unlock new opportunities for growth, efficiency, and innovation.

To stay ahead in the AI race, businesses must:
- Address implementation challenges by prioritizing AI integration and training.
- Reskill the workforce to ensure employees are prepared for the AI-powered workplace.
- Foster a culture of continuous innovation and experimentation.
- Collaborate with AI technology providers and participate in innovation ecosystems to stay at the forefront of AI developments.

By taking these steps, organizations can not only adapt to the rapidly evolving technological landscape but also thrive in it. The future of business is AI-driven, and those who seize the opportunities presented by Generative AI will lead the way.

Vision for AI-Driven Business Transformation

Generative AI is set to become one of the most transformative technologies of the 21st century. Over the next decade, we will see AI permeate every aspect of business, from operations and customer service to marketing and product development.

The most successful companies will be those that harness the power of AI to enhance human creativity, improve decision-making, and deliver personalized experiences at scale.

As AI continues to evolve, it will not only change the way businesses operate but will redefine industries. Companies that embrace AI will not just survive—they will thrive.

The future is bright for organizations that are willing to take bold steps toward AI adoption, and the possibilities are endless for those who lead the charge into this new era of business transformation.

Love & Peace..

Nischal Kapoor

www.ingramcontent.com/pod-product-compliance
Lightning Source LLC
LaVergne TN
LVHW010040070326
832903LV00071B/4442